NONE
DARE
CALL
IT
TREASON!

BOOK 7

Subversives Close
To
Our Presidents

Robert W. Pelton
$4.95

"Treason doth never prosper,

"What's the reason?

"Why if it prosper,

"None dare call it treason."

John Harrington

Printed in America
On Recycled Paper
In
Charleston, South Carolina

Published in America
By
The Freedom & Liberty
Foundation Press
Knoxville, Tennessee

Dedicated
To
My Beloved
America

The greatest, most generous, most benevolent and most powerful nation on the face of the earth – and the only country in the history of the world to have been founded on Biblical principles.

A nation can survive its fools, and even the ambitious. But it cannot survive treason from within.

An enemy at the gates is less formidable, for he is known and he carries his banners openly.

The traitor moves among those within the gates freely, his sly whispers rustling through the galleys, heard in the very hall of government itself.

For the traitor appears not traitor. He speaks in the accent familiar to his victims, and he wears their face and their garments, and he appeals to the baseness that lies deep in the hearts of all men.

He rots the soul of a nation - he works secretly and unknown in the night to undermine the pillars of a city - he infects the body politic so that it can no longer resist.

A murderer is less to be feared.

Cicero, 42 B.C.

CONTENTS

Forward

Independence Hall Where the Declaration of Independence Was Signed.

Our glorious Declaration of Independence is a timeless divinely inspired masterpiece given to mankind through the anointed pen of Thomas Jefferson.

The grand and unmatched United States Constitution is indisputably the product of Providential guidance and wisdom and certainly not a document which evokes whimsical interpretations with the changing political climates.

All Americans have a moral obligation to stand up and be counted in these trying times!

Abraham Lincoln boldly declared: *"To sin by silence when they should protest, makes cowards of men."*

William Lloyd Garrison capsulized it best: *"As a free man who is determined to remain free -- I do not wish to think or speak, or write with moderation. "Tell a man whose house is on fire to give a moderate alarm; tell him to moderately rescue his wife from the hands of a ravisher; tell the mother to gradually extricate her babe from the fire into which it has fallen -- but urge me not to use moderation in a course like the present."*

Senator Barry Goldwater, 1964 Presidential candidate was castigated and verbally crucified by the media.

He simply stated this simple truism: *"Extremism in the pursuit of Liberty is no vice."*

This good and moral man of character soundly rocked the boat of the propagandists. He was as a result soundly defeated in the election.

The alarmed media wolves panicked the voters with their jeers and sneers and insane howls about this man's lack of *"moderation!"*

It can honestly be said that through the Providential genius of our Founding Fathers, the remaining remnants of the original American Constitutional Republic still provides more freedom, opportunity and abundance for mankind than is found in any other nation in the world.

This is true despite decade after decade of unabated treason and treachery promulgated by innumerable traitorous individuals found buried in the twiddle dee – twiddle dum administrations of both the Democrats and the Republicans.

 An informed and active, not a media brainwashed electorate, is the only antidote to further prostitution of, and the ultimate destruction of, what Benjamin Franklin called our Republic.

Preface

"Treason against the United States shall consist only in levying war against them, or in adhering to their enemies, giving them aid and comfort."

U.S. Constitution. Article 111, Section 3

What is your treason I.Q.?

If you can answer the following questions, it's high.

If you miss one or more, you should read the *None Dare Call It Treason* series!

Who was behind allowing Red Chinese soldiers take airborne training at Fort Benning, Georgia?

Is this not treason?

Why was South Vietnam, South Africa, Rhodesia and numerous other American friends deliberately betrayed to the forces of evil?

Is this not treason?

Why was our friend Chiang Kai Shek not so gently coerced into a Communist dictatorship by highly placed subversives in the State Department?

Is this not treason?

Why was Cuba treasonously delivered into the clutches of Communist revolutionary Fidel Castro?

Is this not treason?

Why have untold millions of dollars consistently been used to prop up faltering Red dictatorships and to assist Communist terrorists in overthrowing non-Communist governments?

Is this not treason?

What American company sold nuclear reactors to Communist Occupied Romania?

Is this not treason?

Name the company that provided Communist Hungary with a factory designed to make 1.5 million light bulbs daily?

Is this not treason?

What well known oil company invested $1 billion for oil exploration in Communist Occupied Angola?

Is this not treason?

Can you name the American company who treasonously built and equipped a $10 million electronics plant near Warsaw for the Polish slave labor tyranny?

Is this not treason?

These are questions to which every American should rightfully have an honest answer.

Unfortunately most do not!

Tragedy was carefully orchestrated by traitors in our Government and the media with regard to Cuba, Vietnam, Laos, Cambodia, Rhodesia, China, El Salvador, Nicaragua and many other countries.   Anastasio   Somoza was the former President of free Nicaragua.

He offered this startling insight in his 1980 book, Nicaragua Betrayed: *"I have factual evidence that the betrayal of Nicaragua was not perpetrated out of ignorance, but rather by design."*

Somoza was soon after assassinated!

Is this not treason?

John Lehman, Secretary of the Navy, made this shocking statement on May 25 to the 1983 Annapolis graduating class: *"Within weeks many of you will be looking across just hundreds of feet of water at some of the most modern technology ever invented in America.*

"Unfortunately, it is on Soviet ships."

Is this not treason?

Earl E.T. Smith was the American Ambassador to Cuba when it was similarly delivered to the Communists.

He makes this concise comment on July 14, 1986: *"Nicaragua is Cuba all over again."*

Can you name the company that paid the Communist dictatorship in Angola over $600 million annually in taxes and oil royalties.

This money bought new Soviet jets, tanks and helicopter gunships.

And it paid Castro for supplying 35,000 imported Cuban mercenaries who keep the Angolan people enslaved.

Is this not treason?

Stressed retired Brigadier General Andrew J. Gatsis on August 11, 1986: *"Though aware of the Communist goal of world domination, the average U.S. Citizen refuses to believe that the real threat comes from governmental officials and their non-governmental confederates who secretly espouse the same objectives as the openly avowed Communists."*

 Anthony Sutton stated in his 1986 book *The Best Enemy Money Can Buy: "We now have the formidable task of bringing these gentlemen to the bar of justice to publicly answer for their private and*

concealed actions."

The *None Dare Call It Treason* series certainly won't win accolades from the United Nations or the State Department!

Nor will Harvard feel compelled to bestow an honorary degree upon the author!

Harvard Law School was the spawning ground for an incredible number of Red agents. Included were members of the first Soviet spy ring ever to be exposed in our government.

Reed Irvine aptly commented in July of 1986: *"Indeed, it has long been a joke among refugees from Eastern Europe that there are more Marxists at Harvard than there are in the Soviet Union, or Poland, or whatever Communist country the refugee called home."*

The Honorable Ezra Taft Benson said: *"The truth must be told even at the risk of destroying, in large measure, the influence of*

 men who are widely respected and loved by the American people.

"The stakes are high. Freedom and survival is the issue."

Treason is still a most serious federal offense.

The *None Dare Call It Treason* series examines the reasons for and the Americans behind the fall of freedom and the rise of tyranny throughout the world!

Has anything really changed?
You Decide!

Treason

Whoever, owing allegiance to the United States, levies war against them or adheres to their enemies, giving them aid and comfort within the United States or elsewhere, is guilty of treason and shall suffer death, or be imprisoned not less than five years and fined not less than $10,000; and shall be incapable of holding any office under the United states.

U.S. Code, Title 18, Section 2381

Whoever, owing allegiance to the United States and having knowledge of the commission of any treason against them, conceals and does not, as soon as may be, disclose and make known the same to the President or to some judge of the United States, or to the Governor or to some judge or justice of a particular state, is guilty of misprision of treason, and shall be fined not more than $1000 or imprisoned not more than 7 years or both.

U.S. Code, Title 18, Section 2382

Subversives

Close to

Our

Presidents!

Treason: *"The betrayal of a trust ... breach of faith, treachery to one's country."* **The American College Dictionary**

Presidents come and go but the conspirators working quietly behind the scenes in each Administration often remain.

Thousands of job slots are filled with each change of Presidents.

With whom these openings are staffed largely determines whether or not the Administration follows or thwarts a President's objectives.

A sizable number of positions in every Administration since Roosevelt -- within State, Treasury, Agriculture, the CIA, etc. -- have either been filled with outright Communists, suspected Communists or Communist sympathizers!

Senator William Jenner's 1953 *Senate Internal Security Subcommittee Report* revealed how Russian espionage agents penetrated the government many years ago.

Soviet spies were able to readily obtain jobs all the way up to and including critical policy making positions!

Once secure in a department each Communist mole helped other conspirators find employment.

They placed and promoted their Comrades and helped each other avoid exposure!

Nothing has been done to date with any measurable degree of success to rid the government of these dangerous Moscow hirelings.

Senator Joseph R. McCarthy came too close for comfort!

He was ruthlessly destroyed before his thankless task could be finished.

Congressional hearings have come and gone!

A very few moles have been exposed!

But nothing has been done to force the executive branch to take appropriate action.

A great number of serious security risks began their shadowy careers in government under one President.

They can be traced through succeeding Administrations whether Democrat or Republican!

Important subversives stay behind the scenes to do the bidding of their Kremlin masters.

They avoid controversy.

They work quietly in the background.

They shun the media.

They are often known only to intelligence agencies.

Many names would not be familiar to the average American.

And this is exactly the way it's preferred by a mole.

Moscow directed labor leader Sidney Hillman was extremely close to Roosevelt.

FDR's pat response to questions brought before him?

"Clear it with Sidney."

Hillman was a Communist conspirator.

A Kremlin mole!

And he was President Roosevelt's right-hand man!

This Kremlin espionage agent was President of the Amalgamated Clothing Workers of America.

He was given the job of running the enforcement arm of the National Recovery Administration.

And run it he did!

The NRA was America's first experience with an officially sanctioned Gestapo-like organization!

John T. Flynn recalled: *"They roamed*  *through the garment district like storm troopers.*

"They could enter a man's factory, send him out, line up his employees, subject them to minute interrogation, and take over his books on the instant.

"Night work was forbidden!

"Flying squadrons of these private coat-and-suit police went through the district at night, battering down doors with axes looking for men who were committing the

crime of sewing together a pair of pants at night."

Hillman was adied in the wool Communist spy who'd been deeply and personally involved in the Bolshevik takeover of Russia!

This Kremlin espionage agent was the gave final approval to Harry Truman as Roosevelt's 1944 running mate!

What was a Russian revolutionary from Moscow doing with an important White House job in the first place?

What was a Russian revolutionary from Moscow doing advising an American President?

What traitors already in place were able to maneuver Hillman into this influential position?

Senator Joe McCarthy exposed John J. McCloy (CFR) for approving a shocking order in 1944 while Assistant Secretary of the Army.

His order allowed known Communists to become army officers!

This Harvard security risk worked

closely with other anti-American luminaries at the 1945 UN founding conference.

These included moles such as:

Owen Lattimore

Alger Hiss

Harry Dexter White,

Despite his extensive subversive record McCloy was an advisor to nine Presidents, from Roosevelt to Reagan.

McCarthy rightly charged that McCloy's traitorous career was an *"unbelievable, inconceivable, unexplainable record of the deliberate, secret betrayal of the nation to its mortal enemy, the Communist Conspiracy."*

Harold Ickes became Roosevelt's radical Secretary of the Interior.

This mole in the employ of the Kremlin  brought innumerable Communists into government.

And he was a protector of those already there.

Former Party bigwig Louis Budenz knew Ickes well: *"To his dying day Mr. Ickes defended the 'rights' of the Communist conspiracy and assailed the prosecution of Red leaders under the Smith Act."*

This security risk affiliated himself with numerous Red Fronts and spoke at rallies sponsored by the communist National Council of American-Soviet Friendship.

His wife Jane was also heavily involved in Red activities.

Among other things she was on the National Committee of the Communist founded ACLU.

Security risk David K Niles was another close aid and advisor to Roosevelt.

This Kremlin mole was the White House contact for innumerable Soviet espionage agents.

So close was Soviet mole Harry Hopkins to Roosevelt that he lived in the White House and slept in an adjoining bedroom!

Hopkins was the President's Special Assistant despite his astounding pro-Communist record.

He'd been brought into government at Eleanor Roosevelt's urging!

Harry Hopkins couldn't do enough to help his friends in the Kremlin.

This Kremlin mole authorized the delivery to his Comrades in Communist Occupied Russia of over half of the U.S. uranium supply.

His blatant act of treason was designed to help the Russians develop their own atomic bombs!

With this went cobalt, thorium, and cadmium as well as top secret data from the Manhattan Project.

Perhaps Hopkins believed his treasonous deeds on behalf of his employers in the Russian dictatorship would never be exposed.

Perhaps he didn't care?

He said this in 1941: *"The people are too goddamn dumb to understand!"*

There was only one reason Harry Hopkins wasn't indicted and tried for treason.

He'd already died by the time Congress got around to investigating.

Subversive Assistant Secretary of State Dean Acheson had a protégé named Lauchlin Currie (CFR).

This bespectacled unassuming Kremlin mole became President Franklin Delano Roosevelt's top Administrative Assistant.

Currie was a high-ranking Soviet agent and a member of the Silvermaster spy cell.

When Comrade Currie was called before the House Committee on Un-American Activities his mentor Acheson stepped in as his defense attorney.

Was Acheson another of the deeply buried well protected Kremlin moles?

Security risk Acheson is the same man who had previously vouched for the loyalty of Communist spies Alger and Donald Hiss!

In 1949 Acheson had the audacity to advocate that U.S. Army personnel train Chinese Communist troops!

The lame excuse?

Because Chiang Kai-shek refused to allow Communist participation in his free Chinese government!

Acheson was the man who advised cutting off further arms shipments to Chiang Kai-shek!

His program was designed to disarm the anti-Communist Chinese forces and set the country up for a Red takeover.

Acheson was rewarded well for his traitorous pro-Red, anti-American labors.

Instead of being charged with and tried for treason this blatant security risk was named Truman's Secretary of State in 1949!

Ambassador Arthur Bliss Lane had but one comment: *"God help the United States!"*

President Truman personally selected Michael Greenberg as his top White House assistant.

Greenberg was known to be a member of a Soviet espionage cell was he was identified as a Communist from England's Cambridge University.

Greenberg had been Lauchlin Currie's personal assistant in the Roosevelt White House.

He was finally exposed as a Red espionage agent by Elizabeth Bentley.

"A Republican President will appoint only persons of unquestioned loyalty" proclaimed the Republicans in 1952.

Yet a subversive named Dr. Arthur Flemming became President Eisenhower's Secretary of Health, Education and Welfare!

Flemming consistently decided in favor of identified Communists in government positions while Civil Service Commissioner under President Franklin Roosevelt.

Flemming ruled that Soviet spy Gregory Silvermaster could keep his job despite the serious internal security ramifications!

"Silvermaster was born of a Jewish family in Odessa, Russia, on October 27, 1898,´ reported Wikipedia. *"He moved with*  *his family to China, where he learned to speak perfect English with a British accent,*

"He immigrated to the U.S., and received a B.A. from the University of Washington in Seattle where he was stated to be a known Communist!

"He was reported to be in contact with a very large number of Communist Party USA officials, and was active in a number of Communist front groups.

"Silvermaster denied any Communist links and appealed to overrule the security officials."

 *"Both White House advisor Lauchlin Currie (identified in Venona as the Soviet agent operating under the cover name "Page" and Assistant Secretary of the Treasury Harry Dexter White (identified in Venona as the Soviet agent*

40

operating under the cover names "Lawyer;"
"Jurist"; "Richard" intervened on his behalf.
"Silvermaster subsequently received
two promotions and pay raises."

On May 26, 1953, Senator William Jenner notified President Eisenhower about a serious breach of U.S. security.

The American Communications Association was found to be under total Communist control!

This union was responsible for servicing all communication lines to and from American military bases in the U.S. and overseas!

Eisenhower and his people chose to ignore the warning!

A report was issued which concluded: *"The control that the American Communications Association, a Communist-directed union, maintains over communication lines vital to the national defense poses a threat to the security of this country."*

Still no action was taken!

A little more than three years later, the Senate Internal Security Subcommittee investigated further and issued another report.

William Brucker, Eisenhower's Secretary of the Army, was questioned by Committee counsel Richard Arens.

"Arens: Are you conversant with the fact that the North Atlantic Cable which carries important messages vital to the security of our nation is now serviced by the American Communications Association, a Communist-controlled labor organization?

"Sec. Brucker: I am aware of that."

Brucker offered to do nothing to correct this dangerous security problem!

Eisenhower predictably acted exactly as could be expected when it came to security-related situations.

He too did nothing!

Some congressmen lacked the necessary courage to take remedial action.

Others simply didn't care!

This serious breach of American security still exists today!

Said former congressman William M. Tuck:  *"It is a shocking fact that the North Atlantic cable which day by day carries important, top-secret information to and from the Pentagon itself is being serviced right now by the American Communications Association, a Communist dominated union that was thrown out of the CIO in 1950 because of Communist content."*

Eisenhower's Attorney General Brownell publicly revealed that Truman's Assistant Secretary of the Treasury Harry Dexter White was a Soviet espionage agent.

And that President Truman unquestionably knew of White's spying activities for the Kremlin.

Brownell reported: *"Harry Dexter White was a Russian spy. He smuggled secret*

43

documents to Russian agents for transmission to Moscow.

"Harry Dexter White was known to be a Communist spy by the very people who appointed him to the most sensitive and important position he ever held in Government service.

"The FBI became aware of White's espionage activities and from the beginning made reports on these activities to the appropriate officials in authority. But these reports did not impede White's advancement.

"I can now announce officially for the first time that White's spying activities for the Soviet Government were reported in detail by the FBI to the White House by means of a report delivered to President Truman through his military aide, Brigadier General Harry H. Vaughan, in December of 1945."

Although having been exposed as a Soviet spy White was still able to keep his influential position in the Treasury Department!

And on January 23, 1946, Truman (CFR), all the while knowing White was a spy, nominated him for an even more important higher paying job!

Incredible though it may seem, HST promoted a man he'd been repeatedly warned was an enemy spy!

And the Senate hastily confirmed this Communist agent without debate!

Yes, Harry Dexter White became Executive  Director of the International Monetary Fund!

This known Soviet agent then got the President to appoint his friend Virginius Frank Coe a Kremlin mole as Secretary of the IMF!

William P. Rogers' predecessor Attorney General Herbert Brownell Jr. declared: *"The evidence shows that the National Lawyers Guild is at present a Communist dominated and controlled organization fully committed to the Communist Party line."*

Upon becoming Eisenhower's Attorney General in 1952, Rogers brazenly showed his leftist stripes.

He reversed Brownell and blatantly dropped the Communist NLG from the Attorney General's list of subversive organizations.

The NLG had been cited as *"the foremost legal bulwark of the Communist Party."*

Furthermore, the NLG *"since its inception has never failed to rally to the legal defense of the Communist Party and individual members thereof including known espionage agents."*

Rogers simply chose to ignore the evidence and charged that sufficient proof wasn't available.

He lied!

This subversive became Secretary of State in 1961 during Nixon's first term.

He never veered from his commitment to the Communist cause in America!

The man responsible for Richard Nixon's selection as Ike's running mate in 1952 was notorious leftist Paul Hoffman (CFR).

This security risk was a trustee of the Communist-controlled Institute of Pacific Relations.

The IPR was cited as an instrument of Communist policy, propaganda and military intelligence.

 Hoffman was a member of Eisenhower's Palace Guard who also took part in the conspiracy to silence Senator McCarthy because he was so successfully exposing Reds in government.

Another Harvard leftist, Robert Strange McNamara brought in an array of security risks to traitorously and unilaterally disarm the United States under both the Kennedy and Johnson Administrations.

According to Admiral Chester Ward, McNamara (CFR) deliberately cut back *"90 percent of our nuclear fire power."*

McNamara's radical disarming program charged Ward *"would ultimately lead to a Soviet attack and national suicide."*

Admiral Ward aptly described the CFR when he declared: *"The main purpose of the Council on Foreign Relations is promoting the disarmament of U.S. sovereignty and national independence and submergence into an all powerful, one world government."*

Robert S. Allen and Paul Scott reported: *"Since McNamara became civilian head of the Pentagon in 1961, this country's all-important nuclear weapons stockpile has steadily decreased every year with the full knowledge and approval of the late President Kennedy and President Johnson."*

Daniel Ellsberg (CFR) was another Kissinger protégé and the thief who stole the Pentagon Papers.

This leftist was one of the so-called McNamara *"whiz kids"* who was hired on the recommendation of notorious subversive Adam Yarmolinsky.

Despite everything the media widely heralded McNamara as a *"responsible conservative."*

They weren't joking!

A rather inconspicuous young man named James Burnham was always reverently referred to as an intellectual by his leftist admirers and Communist cohorts.

He was raised Roman Catholic but became a fervent atheist while attending Princeton and Oxford.

Burnham was known to be a leading Trotskyite during the 1930s.

He founded the innocent enough sounding Socialist Worker Party – actually a thoroughly Communist run organization.

Astounding as it may seem this so called *"intellectual"* went from being a Roman Catholic to an atheist and to a rabid Communist leader.

Now we are told to believe Burnham had another amazing turnaround and supposedly had another change of heart.

He suddenly decided to be an anti-Communist rather than a Communist!

Sound like an intellectual?

No!

More like a confused ineffectual individual!

Incredulously there were many in the so-called conservative movement who had despised him but now foolishly and unquestionably embraced him.

Burnham became best known as the *"former"* Trotskyite Communist and editor of the popular *National Review* magazine.

This was published by widely heralded and self impressed conservative leader William F. Buckley (CFR).

And James Burnham boldly informed Americans that he believed notorious Harvard leftist and President John F. Kennedy's Secretary of Defense Robert Strange McNamara was a *"conservative"*.

On December 5, 1960, delegates representing Communist Parties from 81 countries gathered in Moscow.

A manifesto was issued calling for the total destruction of anti-Communism within the United States!

A virulent, carefully orchestrated hate campaign started soon after.

The Communist *People's World* initiated it all by attacking the anti-Communist John Birch Society.

Media leftists of all stripes immediately began parroting Moscow's smears!

Edward Hunter was a widely known psychological warfare expert who appeared before the SISS.

He explained how the Soviets had originated the vicious smear campaign against anti-Communists.

Few people listened!

The Kremlin, Hunter said, viewed the fast growth of anti-Communism in America with a great deal of alarm!

Few people listened!

The Moscow based program explained Hunter was specifically designed to destroy the burgeoning grass roots movement in the United States.

Few people listened!

President Kennedy shamelessly ignored Hunter's warning and joined the Red-planned assault on anti-Communists!

Blatantly following Moscow's directive and spouting the Communist line without deviation JFK first attacked American anti-Communists on November 18, 1961: *"The discordant voices of extremism are heard once again in the land!*

"Men who are unable to face up to the danger from without are convinced that the real danger comes from within.

"They look suspiciously at their neighbors and their leaders. "They find treason in our finest churches, in our highest court!

"But you and I and most Americans take a different view of our peril.

"We know that it comes from without, not within. "

President John F. Kennedy was advised by leftist Walt Rostow that Russian leaders considered U.S. planes, missile bases and first strike weapons to be *"provocative"* and *"worrisome."*

Kennedy quickly responded by stopping Cruise missile deployment!

The Skybolt missile was scrapped,

52

as was the Nike-Zeus anti-missile program for America's defense!

Production of the most remarkable jet fighter plane ever produced by America, the LockheedF-104, was halted!

The Strategic Air Command was to be eliminated!

The RS-70 Bomber was canceled, while the B- 52 and B-58 manned bombers were phased out!

Offensive weapons were destroyed and missile bases abandoned in an insane effort to appease Communist Occupied Russia's slave labor dictatorship!

Dr. Walt Whitman Rostow (CFR) was an atrocious security risk who constantly preached surrender of U.S. sovereignty!

He advocated the absorption of the United States into a world government.

This dictatorship was to be policed and ruled by the Communist-conceived and Communist-controlled United Nations!

Benedict Arnold only tried to surrender the fort at West Point to the British and was severely punished for treason.

Rostow and many clones of his ilk have tried to surrender the entire American nation!

Yet, not one of these traitors has ever even been accused of treason!

Congressman and patriot James B. Utt wrote: *"In January 1962, there was the secret Rostow-Moscow Report which called for the implementation of the 'no-win' policy through the following five points:*

"1. Abandon first strike weapons;

"2. Refrain from encouraging revolts behind the Iron Curtain;

"3. Refrain from criticizing satellite countries;

"4. Deny foreign aid to countries which refuse 'coalition governments';

"5. Work toward general and complete disarmament."

Otto F. Otepka of the State Department security division was pressured by both Rusk and Robert Kennedy in 1961 to clear Rostow.

Otepka adamantly refused!

His decision was based on damaging reports from the FBI, CIA, and Air Force Intelligence.

Two of Rostow's aunts were members of the Communist Party!

His father had been a Russian revolutionary!

Rostow had already been denied a clearance in 1955 and 1957 because of his intimate ties to Soviet spies!

Rostow couldn't be given a security clearance under the terms of *Executive Order 10450.*

This order required that if any question existed as to an applicant's loyalty the doubts were to be resolved in favor of the United States and never to the person in question!

JFK circumvented a security check by giving Rostow a job as Deputy Special Assistant to the President and later elevating him to Chief of the State Department's Policy Planning Council in November of 1961.

Rostow became Johnson's top advisor for National Security Affairs in April of 1966 and headed the National Security Council.

Ironically Rostow couldn't work for the

NSC as a consultant a decade earlier because of his pro-Communist background!

Now he was deliberately catapulted into the top echelons of the government without *any* kind of security check!

As a result one of the most dangerous subversives in America went on to traitorously orchestrate the disastrous no-win Vietnam War from his White House office!

No one has been able to positively prove that Walt Whitman Rostow was a Communist mole.

Reds don't carry cards anymore.

Nor are membership lists readily available.

Whether he was or not is beside the point!

The important question is this: What was anyone with such an astounding Communist tainted background doing making

foreign policy for the United States from 1961 to 1969?

Equally as strange was the later Nixon-Rostow arrangement, exposed by columnist Paul Scott:

"Rostow receives regular secret policy

briefings on foreign and domestic affairs and has access to some of the most sensitive information in government."

Why?

USAF General Thomas Power wrote a book after retiring as head of the Strategic Air Command.

He sent the required 13 manuscript copies to the Pentagon for approval.

Clearance wasn't forthcoming and Power requested their return.

He received only twelve!

The missing copy happened to be the one assigned to Adam Yarmolinsky who was Kennedy's subversive Assistant Secretary of Defense.

Yarmolinsky's copy mysteriously surfaced in Moscow.

This was discovered when Marshall Vasily Danilovich Sokolovsky's *Soviet Military Strategy* was found to contain footnotes referring to Power's unpublished manuscript!

Exactly how the General Power's manuscript found its way to Communist Occupied Russia hasn't ever been clarified!

Why has no one dared asked Comrade Yarmolinsky?

John J. McCloy (CFR) became Kennedy's Special Advisor on Disarmament.

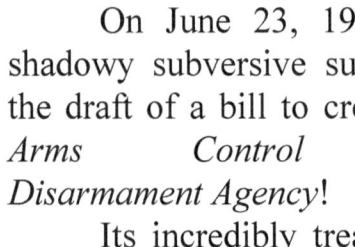

On June 23, 1961 this shadowy subversive submitted the draft of a bill to create the *Arms Control and Disarmament Agency*!

Its incredibly treasonous goals per a McCoy letter to the President were to disarm the United States; turn American weapons over to a UN militia; and bring about world government!

In September 1961, Congress actually passed the suicidal *Arms Control and Disarmament Act*!

Congressman James Utt revealed that the plagiarized legislation was an *"almost word-for-word duplication of a disarmament proposal advanced by Khrushchev in 1959."*

The *Arms Control and Disarmament Act* was later published as a 19-page report entitled *Freedom From War: United States Program for General and Complete Disarmament in a Peaceful World.*

It should have read *Freedom from War: Moscow's Program for the Disarming and Surrender of the United States.*

The plan was for the United States to disarm unilaterally!

In other words America was to disarm whether or not the Communist enemy disarms!

Under McCloy's legislation all nuclear testing was to stop!

No nuclear weapons were to be produced!

No missile delivery systems were to be manufactured!

No systems were to be built to defend the U.S. against enemy missile attacks!

Existing nuclear warheads and all U.S. military forces eventually were to be transferred to the Communist controlled UN!

Texas Senator John Tower took issue with the plan: *"As skeptical as I have always been of the measure of loyalty within the State Department I never would have believed our diplomats could so completely and unabashedly advocate the surrender of*  *American rights and sovereignty!*

"If more American people knew about this scheme there would be a nationwide uproar that would make the reaction to the Alger Hiss scandal look like another era of good feeling by comparison!"

Unfortunately the American people were never told!

Not surprisingly the media did amazingly little to publicize this treasonous activity at the highest levels of government!

Therefore, no uproar was ever heard from the public.

This insane disarming plan and the resulting surrender of U.S. sovereignty is still  quietly being adhered to almost three decades later!

Security risk Theodore C. Sorensen (CFR) was deeply involved in the treacherous Kennedy betrayal of the heroic anti-Communist Cuban freedom fighters, at the Bay of Pigs in April 1961!

He avidly denounced all government loyalty and internal security programs!

He called for disarming America!

And he took classified documents from the White House without authorization!

Sorensen advocated the dismantling of American's foreign intelligence gathering apparatus!

He was in the forefront of the surrender-appeasement mob!

Berserk leftists were howling for a bombing halt and negotiations with Communist Occupied North Vietnam which would allow them to more easily take over the South!

This subversive was bitter over the controversy brought about by Carter trying to install him as CIA Director.

Taking the textbook leftist approach, Sorensen charged that he'd been smeared by *"the extreme right wing."*

The man's atrocious pro-Communist record had simply been made public by Congressman Larry McDonald.

McGeorge Bundy had the same job later held by identified Kremlin espionage agent Henry Kissinger under President Nixon!

And by an avowed Marxist named Zbigniew Brzezinski under President Carter!

A protégé of suspected communist spy Dean Acheson, Dean Rusk's disloyalty was never a secret!

The *"liberal"* media had the audacity to label him a *"hardline anti-Communist"*.

Their absurd attempt to ignore this security risk's atrocious pro-Communist record was almost laughable!

Rusk (CFR) brought a multitude of subversives into the State Department and purged it of anti-Communists.

There is no question that Dean Rusk deliberately aided Communist Occupied

Russia in expanding its extensive spy network throughout the government.

Communists and suspected Reds were now warmly welcomed to the White House.

Included were Communist Linus Pauling and J. Robert Oppenheimer who'd his clearance revoked because of his Communist affiliations.

Willard Wirtz was another serious security risk.

He became JFK's new Labor Secretary on the recommendation of leftist Arthur Goldberg.

Willard's brother Robert once headed a group collecting signatures in order to get the Communist Party on the ballot in Illinois.

Feature columnist Ed Montgomery had this to say: *"On this detail was a brother, William W. Wirtz.*

"William is no longer known by that name.

"Today he is better known as W. Willard Wirtz, Secretary of Labor of the United States."

Assistant Secretary of Labor was Esther Peterson!

This woman was suspected of being a member of the Communist Party.

 Her security file revealed close associations over a long period of years with Reds and Red sympathizers.

The White House social calendar as well had numerous dinners and receptions in honor of brutal communist dictators.

These included Yugoslavia's Tito and Sekou Toure, Guinea's own version of the horrid "Big Daddy" Idi Amin.

In 1965 the Johnson Administration was going full steam ahead in treasonously bankrolling, assisting, feeding and arming dire Communist enemies of the U.S.

Top American research facilities were regularly toured by groups of Red Bloc scientists!

One such *"scientific"* expedition included representatives from Communist Occupied Romania, Poland, Czechoslovakia, Yugoslavia and Hungary.

Each Red dictatorship was an openly professed ally and supplier of military aid to the enemy North Vietnamese Communist forces!

Congressman Richard Roudebush revealed how these Iron Curtain experts were allowed to *"lecture, conduct seminars, survey our current research, take field trips in the U.S., and conduct research of their own."*

These Communist Bloc scientists were even paid a salary while they were in the United States!

American taxpayers were footing the bill for everything!

These ludicrous trips were allowed to take place even though intelligence data proved that most Red Bloc scientists allowed to visit the U.S. were KGB agents!

Even those few who aren't were given assignments by the KGB to obtain specific classified materials!

FBI Director J. Edgar Hoover explained: *"Upon returning, Soviet scientists who have visited the United States under the exchange program are required by the KGB to submit comprehensive reports on the technical aspects of their trip, including descriptions of installations*  *visited, research being conducted, and the status of particular projects.*

"They must also submit reports concerning Americans contacted, for possible future use by the KGB."

Richard Nixon signed an agreement with Communist Occupied Russia's Leonid Brezhnev that stated its objectives were *"general and complete disarmament."*

President Nixon was well aware that a Communist always commanded the UN military forces!

This came about per an understanding reached many years ago between Stalin and

Roosevelt at the infamous Yalta Conference!

Alger Hiss was the President's shadow at Yalta and advised him on every issue!

Yet President Nixon still was willing to treasonously agree to the establishment of an all-powerful UN land, sea and air forces which would surpass that of the United States!

Along with this travesty Nixon also had concrete plans to declare martial law when necessary to subdue any internal disorders!

He was rightfully accused by William Howard of the Newhouse newspaper chain of *"making plans for a dictatorship in America."*

Lyndon Baines Johnson assumed the Presidency in November of 1963.

The first person he called was the ghoulish Neanderthal monster Nikita Khrushchev in Moscow.

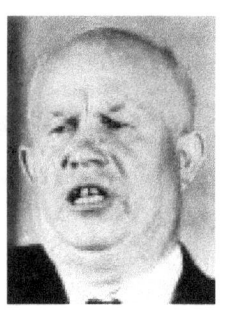

This wasn't done to break diplomatic relations as he should have!

After all Oswald was known by American intelligence to be a Soviet trained assassin who'd married into a KGB family!

Johnson wasn't a man to easily scare!
But he thought he might be the next target.
The President needed to have the world's worst mass-murderer's assurance that he wasn't.
The second person Johnson called for even more reassurance was his old Communist buddy Aubrey Williams.

 Before first running for Congress in 1937 LBJ had been State Director of the New Deal's Red-riddled Youth Administration In Texas.

His Washington boss was Communist Party member Aubrey Williams who later endorsed him for Congress!
Williams was a member of the Communist-founded ACLU and Chairman of the National Committee to Abolish the Un-American Activities Committee.

He was a close friend of Marxist revolutionary Martin Luther King.

Their association went back to the days when they attended the Highlander Folk School a Communist training facility in Monteagle, Tennessee!

Radical leftist Pro-North Vietnam anti-American Ramsey Clark replaced security risk Nicholas deB Katzenbach as Johnson's Attorney General in 1967.

This radical leftist was with the KGB controlled International Association of Democratic Lawyers! The IADL was cited as being *"One of the most useful Communist Front organizations at the service of the Soviet Communist Party"*.

Clark (CFR) refused to prosecute Reds and other traitors under the existing *Trading with the Enemy Act* and the *Export-Import Control Act.*

Therefore, it wasn't a crime in the eyes of this subversive Attorney General to solicit supplies (blood, ammunition, money, food,

69

arms, etc.) for the enemy in Communist Occupied Hanoi.

Clark even refused to indict Communist terrorist Stokely Carmichael and Marxist race  agitator Martin Luther King when they publicly urged defiance of the *Selective Service Act*!

This law specifies penalties for any person *"who knowingly counsels, aids or abets another to refuse or evade registration for service in the Armed Forces."*

Clark irrationally argued it would be a violation of their *"free speech"* to prosecute!

Gary Allen charged: *"Frankly, if Stokely Carmichael is not guilty of sedition, then the Communists have already destroyed our sedition laws.*

"If he cannot be convicted for giving 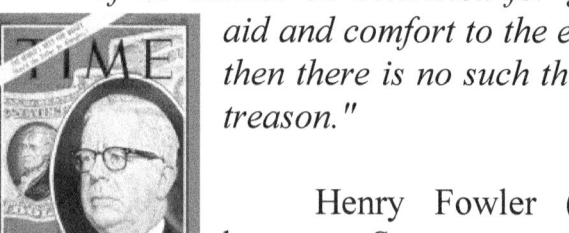 *aid and comfort to the enemy, then there is no such thing as treason."*

Henry Fowler (CFR) became Secretary of the Treasury.

He'd been Virginia chairman of the Southern Conference for Human Welfare.

This organization was cited as the South's top Communist front!

Fowler was responsible for getting Communist espionage agent and member of the Perlo cell Harry Samuel Magdoff an influential government job.

Magdoff held several administrative positions in government during the presidency of Franklin D. Roosevelt.

He lied regarding his employment in order to obtain a job as an economist with several New Deal agencies.

During World War II as Chief Economist on the War Production Board Magdoff passed much classified information to the Soviet Union.

Magdoff was a dues paying member of the Communist Party USA.

At the time the law forbade employment within the United States Government of persons belonging to groups which advocated the violent overthrow of our Constitutional form of government

Kremlin spy Charles Flato mentioned Fowler prominently while testifying before the SISS.

Red agent Irving Kaplan was also a member of the Perlo spy ring as well as Silvermaster's.

Kaplan was asked when he knew Henry Fowler.

The man replied: *"I refuse to answer on the grounds that it may tend to incriminate me."*

Wilbur J. Cohen was a self-professed Marxist who drafted the original *Social Security* laws in 1935!

Known as the *"Father of Medicare"* this Kremlin mole worked for two decades to force socialized medicine on America.

According to former Congressman Martin Dies the passage of *Medicare* in 1965 was the most monumental advancement toward a Communist state in American history!

Cohen belonged to many Communist fronts and he was close to top Red agents over a long period of years.

Dr. Marjorie Shearon has this to say about her former colleague: *"Those investigating in Congress and the FBI were very close in the 1950s.*

"Men like Pressman, Stern and Kramer were confessing, or being proven, to have been Communists.

` *"These were the men Cohen had worked with and who had helped him in his legislative achievements."*

Despite all the incriminating evidence security risk Cohen was welcomed back in government by LBJ.

He was appointed to be Johnson's Secretary of Health, Education and Welfare in 1968!

Incredible?

Yes!

But true!

Stewart Udall was Secretary of Interior under both Kennedy and Johnson.

This leftist believed that private ownership of property was outmoded.

He had the audacity to give his idol Communist Woody Guthrie the Conservation Service Award for 1966.

Udall also had the gall to honor revolutionary Eugene V. Debs by making his home a *"national historic landmark!"*

Debs was an apologist for Lenin's ruthless mass murder of his countrymen.

He was a subversive who was once tried and convicted for sedition!

Ironically, under the Reagan Administration in 1988 landmark status was *denied* for the Maryland farm of former Communist Whittaker Chambers who had been instrumental in exposing Alger Hiss and numerous other Soviet spies!

Robert Weaver another Harvard cloned security risk became President Johnson's head of Housing and Urban Development (HUD) in 1966.

He started out in 1933 as an economic advisor to subversive Secretary of Interior Harold L. Ickes who was a notoriously rabid defender of the Red conspiracy.

Weaver then became an Administrative Assistant to Russian spy Sidney Hillman on the National Defense Advisory Committee.

There are few people in government who were better qualified through experience to serve the interests of Moscow!

Weaver was a leader at the second National Negro Congress in 1937, cited as *"the Communist front movement in the United States among Negroes."*

He was also a member of the Washington Book Shop Association which was cited as being *"So obviously an enterprise of the Communist Party that it would have been impossible for any politically informed person to walk into it without perceiving its Communist character."*

Much of Richard Nixon's early political career was built on his undeserved reputation as an anti-Communist!

He gained some measure of fame as a Congressman in the sensational Communist spy scandal involving Alger Hiss.

Nixon chose leftist Joseph E. Johnson (CFR) to be one of his Administration's talent scouts.

Johnson was a close friend and chief State Department assistant of Kremlin espionage agent Alger Hiss.

He'd also been President of the pro-Communist Carnegie Endowment for International Peace.

The subversive Carnegie organization had been headed by Soviet spy Hiss from 1946 to 1949 even though the trustees had known of his Communist spying activities before he was given the job.

Another of Nixon's major talent scouts was Harvard subversive Adam Yarmolinsky (CFR).

This security risk had also helped select the entire Kennedy cabinet.

Congressman Nixon Showing the Incriminating Microfilm that Confirmed Whttaker Chamber's Testimony About Kremlin Agent Alger Hiss.

Yarmolinsky was the son of two Communists!

He once headed the Harvard Marxist Club and edited the *Yardling* which was the official campus voice of the Young Communist League!

This subversive told investigators: *"The Young Communist league believed, and I was inclined to believe that a so-called Communist government was a desired end."*

Despite all these things, Yarmolinsky became leftist Robert McNamara's top advisor and an influential behind-the-scenes policymaker!

Yarmolinsky's Communist track record was reviewed by State Department Chief Security Officer Raymond A. Laughton.

He adamantly refused to grant a security clearance.

Laughton resigned when his decision was overruled by *"higher authority."*

Yarmolinsky's notorious subversive career in government since his Communist-oriented days at Harvard revealed nothing to show that his views had changed one iota!

Nevertheless, this man became one of security risk Paul Warnke's assistants on the

Arms Control and Disarmament Agency under Carter.

Communist fronter James Farmer became top assistant to the Secretary of Health, Education and Welfare.

This subversive had been Vice-President of the Marxist League for Industrial Democracy!

He was a board member of Tom Hayden's Communist led Students for a Democratic Society and the Communist founded ACLU!

Farmer's name could be found on the National Executive Board of the American Committee on Africa that inexcusably supported Red terrorists and their murderous activities!

The notoriously subversive Dean Acheson was also believed to be a spy in the employ of Communist Occupied Russia.

This untouchable radical leftist was constantly berated by Congressman Richard Nixon over his radical words and deeds.

Yet on September 28, 1969, Walter  Cronkite did a television special that whitewashed Acheson's pro-Communist career.

It was here that Acheson revealed he was serving President Nixon as an advisor!

President Gerald Ford personally selected another identified Red to be his Vice President!

CIA Director Walter Bedell Smith *"warned Eisenhower that Rockefeller was a Communist"* in the 1950s.

When Nelson Rockefeller was Assistant Secretary of State in 1944-1945 he was given incriminating files by the FBI.

These files proved beyond and reasonable that Alger Hiss and Harry Dexter White were Soviet moles!

Rockefeller is reported to have personally destroyed this irrefutable evidence.

He said that he and others in the State Department believed the FBI was *"a Fascist organization in our own midst!"*

We now know that this was no more than a case of a fellow Red mole protecting his Comrades!

Ford was asked on November 14, 1974, about the most notable achievements of his first 100 days as President.

He declared: *"Number one, nominating Nelson Rockefeller!"*

Ford's Attorney General Edward H. Levi had been selected by two identified Communists.

They were Henry Kissinger and Nelson Rockefeller.

This fact alone should tell us something.

Levy was a member of the National Lawyers Guild which was founded by the

Communist Party solely to defend Communists and Communist activities!

While dean of the University of Chicago Law School this subversive hired a fellow Communist to head his law library.

The new employee had been exposed as a member of the Silvermaster spy cell.

How convenient!

Sidney Harman was President Carter's selection to be his Under Secretary of Commerce.

This man was formerly a trustee of the radical leftist Institute of Policy Studies!

The staff of this blatantly pro-Communist think tank included a variety of Marxist-oriented misfits.

There were Communist Party members, KGB operatives, Weather Underground terrorists and leaders of the Trotskyite Fourth International!

Other Carter people connected to the IPS included White House advisor Peter Bourne who was *"the President's closest friend"*, Sam Brown, Margery Tabankin and John Lewis.

Coleman Young was a Communist who became chairman of Carter's 1980 Democratic Platform Committee.

Did the Georgia peanut farmer have brain damage?

Or what?

This Red espionage agent had also been a delegate in 1957 to the American Communist Party Convention.

Young, center, testified before the House Un-American Activities Committee in 1952.

A future House member and fellow subversive George Crockett Jr. can be seen sitting on his right.

Detroit's subversive Mayor was a founder of the Communist National Negro Labor Council.

Young was identified as a leading Negro Communist in the United States.

President Carter chose *"former"* Communist Lawrence R. Klein to be his top economist!

 Klein appeared before the House Committee on Un-American Activities in 1954 and admitted to having once been a Party member.

He claimed to have broken with the Communists!

Why?

Because they were *"dull"*

Klein said he'd rather work for *"socialism"* outside the Party.

Klein taught at important Red training schools in Chicago and Boston which were cited as *"adjuncts of the Communist Party."*

Here we have a highly placed official in the Carter Administration who claimed to have left the Communist Party out of boredom!

But he admittedly continued to work toward the goals of Communism!

This was acceptable to the President of the United States?

Evidently!

One of the most astounding security risks brought into the Reagan Administration was the notorious Kremlin man Armand Hammer.

He was to be an unofficial *"shuttle diplomat to work out a solution to the conflict"* in Afghanistan.

A photo signed by Lenin hung in his office.

His idol wrote: *"To Comrade Armand Hammer."*

Huh?

This subversive's father Dr. Julius Hammer was a founder of the Communist Party USA and an intimate of Lenin.

Armand took tons of supplies to Communist Occupied Russia in 1921 to help the new Red dictatorship get on its feet.

He stayed until 1931.

Hammer presently has an astounding number of business interests in the Soviet Union.

And he's a key figure in the transfer of American technology to these avowed enemies of freedom.

Former Congressman Martin Dies offered this succulent tidbit: *"The Committee on Un-American Activities named not less than five thousand Communists on the federal payroll and fifteen thousand working in defense industries.*

"The Administration fired a few of these people.

"All of them have been rehired.

"We have yet to hear a satisfactory answer to what those five thousand Communists we found were doing in the federal government, unless they were stealing invaluable secrets and influencing our policies."

Anyone attempting to unearth Reds in government today is still charged with *"McCarthyism."*

Such courageous individuals are also derogatorily labeled *"Birchites," "extremists," "rightwing fanatics"* or part of the *"lunatic fringe!"*

These Pavlovian scare words were deliberately coined by Comrades of the very traitors being investigated!

They were designed to elicit a conditioned response and to force concerned patriotic citizens to back off and leave the traitors alone.

This technique has proved to be immensely successful for the Communists and their *"liberal"* patrons, protectors and friends!

Epilogue

The record covering crucial episodes of the McCarthy era has been massively and deliberately distorted from the very beginning!

Conveniently forgotten or deliberately overlooked are the 78 hearings held between 1951 and 1952 by Senator William E. Jenner's (R-Indiana) Senate Internal Security Subcommittee (SISS); the House Committee On Internal Security; the House Un-American Activities Committee (HUAC) under the chairmanship of both Martin Dies (D-Texas) and Francis Walters (D-Pa); the Federal Bureau of Investigation (FBI) under the guidance of J. Edgar Hoover; and other investigating committees and individuals.

Out of all of these investigations one man was selected:

To be stopped!
To be destroyed!
To be made an example!

Why?

So that no one would ever again dare to initiate any investigations into the penetration of our government agencies by communist agents (spies) in the employ of the Soviet Union!

Yes!

An obscure Senator from Wisconsin was deliberately targeted for this purpose!

Joseph McCarthy's incredibly successful investigations panicked those on the political left.

Their reaction was shockingly quick!

Key data was been suppressed, denied and even widely falsified.

This took place in the media, all branches of government and many alleged scholars entrenched in the ivory towers of our institutions of higher learning!

Such misreporting and misrepresentation of the facts continues today.

Much of the misinformation we were (and still are today) so carefully spoon-fed about Senator Joseph McCarthy the man and his investigations was no more than an admixture of uncheckable blovations from deceased third parties and demonstratable falsehoods!

For example, how many innocent people were harmed by McCarthy's revelations?

The correct answer?

Not one!

No!

Not One!

McCarthy's most virulent critics have had more than a half century to produce the names of the hundreds of innocent people they claim were destroyed by the astounding revelations of the Senator from Wisconsin.

Yet those highly skilled propagandists in our media and government and institutions of higher learning have been unable to name even one innocent person they claim was destroyed after being falsely accused by McCarthy!

How many innocent people committed suicide as a result of McCarthy's exposure?

The correct answer?

Not one!

Not one suicide can be attributed to the investigations conducted by McCarthy!

No! Not one!

According to the obscene claims made the highly skilled propagandists in our media, government and scholars entranced in those ivory towers of our colleges and universities there were a rash of suicides with bodies falling constantly of the heads of pedestrians below on the streets of Manhattan!

91

Once again, McCarthy's most virulent critics have had more than 50 years to produce the names of the hundreds of innocent people they claim committed suicide because of the astounding revelations of the Senator from Wisconsin.

Yet those highly skilled propagandists in our media and government and institutions of higher learning have been unable to name even one innocent person they claim committed suicide after being falsely accused by McCarthy!

No!

Not one!

But there were two suicides on record during the McCarthy period!

Neither was the result of an innocent person who'd been ruined by McCarthy's revelations!

Both were subversives who'd been exposed by McCarthy!

Both were subversives who'd been positively indentified as Kremlin agents!

Lawrence Duggan had been operating in the State Department as a widely known Soviet spy!

He'd been called to testify before a Congressional investigating committee.

Duggan never made it!

He conveniently "fell" from a window high up in a Manhattan skyscraper!

Fell?

Probably not!

He was more than likely pushed from or tossed out of the window by an assassin in the employ of the Soviet Union!

Why?

To make certain he didn't fold under pressure and start naming other Kremlin moles.

Secondly there was the unexpected demise of Harry Dexter White.

This Soviet agent discovered that he was being investigated by J. Edgar Hoover of the FBI!

He died of a sudden heart attack!

Coincidence?

Not hardly!

Was White's death a suicide?

Yes or at least so claimed McCarthy's critics!

Again, not hardly!

Heart attacks can readily be induced with the proper use of certain medicines administered by a hired assassin in the employ of the Kremlin!

Why?

Simply to eliminate anyone who might panic and decide to turncoat and reveal the names of other spies secretly entrenched deeply in the bowels of every branch of our government.

To sum up, most fit into one of three categories:

Conscience lacking incurable liars!

Those with an axe to grind!

Individuals who simply do not know the facts!

If you liked this book in the *None Dare Call It Treason* series then you'll probably also enjoy reading the others!

Gift copies of this book can be ordered at

createspace.com/4213931

or robertwpelton.com or amazon.com

Available Titles

None Dare Call It Treason Book 1
The Internal Security Farce!
5.5" x 8.5" 97 pages $4.95
Order from createspace.com/4215951
robertwpelton.com or amazon.com

None Dare Call It Treason Book 2
Never Ending Subversion
In Government!
5.5" x 8.5" 202 pages $4.95
Order from createspace.com/4216385
robertwpelton.com or amazon.com

None Dare Call It Treason Book 3
America's Subversive State Department
Bloated With Security Risks
5.5" x 8.5" 202 pages $4.95
Order from createspace.com/4216626
robertwpelton.com or amazon.com

None Dare Call It Treason Book 4
America's Illustrious State Department!
It's Machiavellian Misdeeds!
5.5" x 8.5" 202 pages $4.95
Order from createspace.com/4215018
robertwpelton.com or amazon.com

None Dare Call It Treason Book 5
Our Presidents A Major Security Threat!
5.5" x 8.5" 202 pages $4.95
Order from createspace.com/4213501
robertwpelton.com or amazon.com

None Dare Call It Treason Book 6
Presidential Words & Deeds &Blatant Lies!
5.5" x 8.5" 202 pages $4.95
Order from createspace.com/4213920
robertwpelton.com or amazon.com

None Dare Call It Treason Book 7
Subversives Close To Our Presidents
5.5" x 8.5" 89 pages $4.95
Order from createspace.com/4213931
robertwpelton.com or amazon.com

None Dare Call It Treason Book 8
Henry Kissinger
The Shadowy Untouchable Kremlin Spy!
5.5" x 8.5" 202 pages $4.95
Order from createspace.com/4214986
robertwpelton.com or amazon.com

None Dare Call It Treason Book 9
Inexcusably Arming America's Enemies!
5.5" x 8.5" 202 pages $4.95
Order from createspace.com/4216634
robertwpelton.com or amazon.com

None Dare Call It Treason Book 10
Inexcusably Financing
America's Enemies!
5.5" x 8.5" 202 pages $4.95
Order from createspace.com/4216777
robertwpelton.com or amazon.com

None Dare Call It Treason Book 11
Treasonous Trade With & Aid To
Enemies Of Freedom!
5.5" x 8.5" 202 pages $4.95
Order from createspace.com/4216873
robertwpelton.com or amazon.com

None Dare Call It Treason Book 12
Wholesale Treason During the War
In Vietnam!
5.5" x 8.5" 202 pages $4.95
Order from createspace.com/4215293
robertwpelton.com or amazon.com

None Dare Call It Treason Book 13
Big Business
& Astounding Acts Of Treason!
5.5" x 8.5" 202 pages $4.95
Order from createspace.com/4215805
robertwpelton.com or amazon.com

None Dare Call It Treason Book 14
Illegally Importing
Slave Made Goodies!
5.5" x 8.5" 202 pages $4.95
Order from createspace.com/4215894
robertwpelton.com or amazon.com

None Dare Call It Treason Book 15
The House That Hiss Built
The Anti-American United Nations!
5.5" x 8.5" 202 pages $4.95
Order from createspace.com/4215323
robertwpelton.com or amazon.com

None Dare Call It Treason Book 16
Security Risks in the House and Senate!
5.5" x 8.5" 202 pages $4.95
Order from createspace.com/4213508
robertwpelton.com or amazon.com

None Dare Call It Treason Book 17
The Supreme Court A Devastating
Threat To National Security!
5.5" x 8.5" 202 pages $4.95
Order from createspace.com/4213689
robertwpelton.com or amazon.com

Orders for Resale
40% Off Retail Price

Send Purchase Order to
christianamerica2@yahoo.com

MEET THE AUTHOR

Robert W. Pelton has been writing and lecturing for more than 45 years on political, religious and historical subjects.

He has published more than 100 books including the sensational exposé *Unwanted Dead or Alive – The Greatest Act of Treason in Our History – The betrayal of American POWs Following World War II, Korea and Vietnam.*

Mr, Pelton proudly claims a heritage going all the way back to well before the War for American Independence.

One of Mr. Pelton's ancestors, John Rogers, came to America on the Mayflower and was one of 41 signers of the Mayflower Compact.

Another, John Smith was one of the founders of Jamestown.

Peleg Pelton served as the fifer in the Continental Army at age 18 during the Battle of Saratoga (1777) and again in Yorktown (1781).

Captain Peter Hager was Commander of the Old Stone Fort in Schoharie, New York, in 1780.

Another, Captain Bezaleel Tyler fought in the only Revolutionary War Battle taking place in Sullivan County, New York.

Mr. Pelton is a member of Sons of the Revolution (SOR), and Sons of the American Revolution (SAR).